# Mandala Coloring

Mandala coloring has emerged as a popular form of therapeutic activity in recent years, captivating individuals of all ages and backgrounds. Originating from the ancient Sanskrit word for "circle," mandalas are intricate geometric designs often representing the universe, wholeness, and harmony. The practice of coloring these elaborate patterns has become a widely recognized method for relaxation, mindfulness, and creative expression.

The process of coloring mandalas encourages individuals to focus their attention on the present moment, allowing worries and stresses to fade away as they immerse themselves in the intricate details of the design. This meditative quality promotes a state of mindfulness, where one becomes fully engaged in the act of coloring, experiencing a sense of calm and inner peace.

Moreover, mandala coloring is not just about filling in spaces with colors; it also involves making choices about which colors to use and how to blend them harmoniously. This aspect of creative decision-making fosters a sense of empowerment and self-expression, as individuals personalize their mandalas according to their unique preferences and emotions.

Furthermore, the repetitive and rhythmic motions involved in coloring mandalas can have a soothing effect on the mind and body, similar to other forms of meditative practices such as yoga or tai chi. This rhythmic activity has been shown to reduce stress levels, lower blood pressure, and promote overall well-being.

Additionally, mandala coloring can be a shared experience, bringing people together in group settings or fostering connections between individuals who share a passion for creativity and self-care. It serves as a bridge for communication and camaraderie, allowing participants to bond over their shared love for art and mindfulness.

In today's fast-paced and often chaotic world, the simple act of coloring mandalas provides a much-needed respite, offering a space for reflection, rejuvenation, and inner exploration. Whether as a form of self-care, a creative outlet, or a means of connecting with others, mandala coloring continues to enchant and inspire individuals on their journey towards balance and tranquility.